YELLOWSTONE

A LAND OF WILD AND WONDER

CHRISTOPHER CAUBLE

RIVERBEND
PUBLISHING

Yellowstone: A Land of Wild and Wonder
Copyright © 2016 Christopher Cauble, www.caublephotography.com
Published by Riverbend Publishing, Helena, Montana

Design by Sarah Cauble, www.sarahcauble.com

ISBN 13: 978-1-60639-092-4

Printed in India

Distributed by NATIONAL BOOK NETWORK

Riverbend Publishing
P.O. Box 5833
Helena, MT 59604
www.riverbendpublishing.com

Front cover photo: Boardwalk, Upper Geyser Basin
Back cover photos: Thermal pattern at Grand Prismatic Spring, bull elk
Title page photo: Gull Point on Yellowstone Lake

In Memory of
Samuel Cooper Howell Sylvester

PRONGHORN

INTRODUCTION

BY CHRISTOPHER CAUBLE

Growing up in Montana, some of my earliest memories were family trips to Yellowstone. We hiked along snowy Slough Creek; backpacked into the isolated Thorofare country; and fished for cutthroat trout deep in the canyons of the Yellowstone River.

Whether it was exploring the gravel shoreline of Yellowstone Lake or the late nights looking up at the stars next to a warm campfire, Yellowstone always filled me with a sense of wonder.

As I grew older, my fascination with the park became a journey of discovery. I came to understand how the natural environment changed as the seasons turned, and I began to see the interwoven patterns of plants and wildlife in a fully functioning, wild ecosystem. I began to see Yellowstone in an intimate way.

After many years of exploring and photographing Yellowstone, I learned, as so many people do, that there's nothing quite like it in the world. The wildlife, geysers, mountains, and rivers all blend to make it a truly special place, a unique whole of wild and wonder.

No matter how many days you spend in Yellowstone, there's always something new to see. Each morning there is excitement and anticipation about what the day will bring. I hope these photographs instill a sense of wonder, and perhaps become part of your Yellowstone discovery.

ELECTRIC PEAK

SANDHILL CRANE

LOWER FALLS OF
THE YELLOWSTONE RIVER

THERMAL STEAM NEAR
MOUNT WASHBURN

BISON AT MIDWAY GEYSER BASIN

BISON

HEART SPRING,
UPPER GEYSER BASIN

THERMAL PATTERN IN
THE UPPER GEYSER BASIN

PENDANT HOT SPRING,
UPPER GEYSER BASIN

COYOTE HOWLING
AT TOWER JUNCTION

WINTER IN THE
NORTHERN RANGE

THERMAL PATTERN AT
GRAND PRISMATIC SPRING

BULL ELK

ABSAROKA RANGE FROM AVALANCHE PEAK

MYSTIC FALLS

SUNSET AT PORCELAIN BASIN,
NORRIS GEYSER BASIN

GRAND PRISMATIC SPRING
FOLLOWING PAGES: BLACK POOL,
WEST THUMB GEYSER BASIN

BOARDWALK, MAMMOTH HOT SPRINGS

CASTLE GEYSER, UPPER GEYSER BASIN

COYOTE ALONG THE YELLOWSTONE RIVER

DUCK LAKE

PRONGHORNS

PRONGHORN SHAKING OFF LOOSE HAIR

ARROWLEAF
BALSAMROOT

INDIAN
PAINTBRUSH

BLACK BEAR CUBS

BISON TRACKS IN BISCUIT BASIN

OLD FAITHFUL GEYSER AND INN
UNDER THE MILKY WAY

BISON IN HAYDEN VALLEY

LOWER FALLS

FOGBOW IN HAYDEN VALLEY

GREAT GRAY OWL

BALANCED ROCK, GIBBON RIVER

SENTINEL CREEK

SODA BUTTE CREEK

GRIZZLY BEAR

CARRINGTON ISLAND, YELLOWSTONE LAKE

UNDINE FALLS

BIGHORN SHEEP RAM

WINTER IN LOWER
GEYSER BASIN

WINTER AT ROUND PRAIRIE

BARRONETTE PEAK
FOLLOWING PAGES: POND
NEAR SLOUGH CREEK

MOUNTAIN
BLUEBIRD

BLUE FUNNEL SPRING,
WEST THUMB GEYSER BASIN

COMMON MERGANSERS FLYING OVER
PARTIALLY FROZEN YELLOWSTONE LAKE

YELLOWSTONE BACKCOUNTRY
FROM THE WASHBURN RANGE

DOUBLE-CRESTED CORMORANT

FROSTY MORNING IN HAYDEN VALLEY

TROUT LAKE

THERMAL PATTERN IN NORRIS GEYSER BASIN

SUNSET LAKE, BLACK SAND BASIN

GRAND GEYSER

BLACK BEAR SOW AND CUB
FOLLOWING PAGES: SUMMER
IN LAMAR VALLEY

RAINBOW AT TOWER JUNCTION

BISON IN HAYDEN VALLEY

PHANTOM LAKE

COW ELK AT SWAN LAKE FLATS

NIGHT SKY NEAR SODA BUTTE CREEK

OLD FAITHFUL

BOARDWALK, WEST THUMB GEYSER BASIN

COW ELK AT WEST THUMB GEYSER BASIN

COMMON RAVEN

PALETTE SPRING, MAMMOTH HOT SPRINGS

CASCADE LAKE

BARRONETTE PEAK

COYOTE

OSPREY ABOVE THE
FIREHOLE RIVER

WILLETS ON THE SHORE OF
YELLOWSTONE LAKE

CANARY SPRING,
MAMMOTH HOT SPRINGS

ANTLER PEAK (RIGHT) AND THE
GALLATIN RANGE, SWAN LAKE FLATS

SUNBURST THROUGH THE TREES
AT MAMMOTH HOT SPRINGS

BULL ELK IN WINTER

SODA BUTTE CREEK

YELLOWSTONE NIGHT SKY

COYOTE AT ROUND PRAIRIE

BISON AND MALLARDS

BULL ELK

ASPENS IN WINTER
FOLLOWING PAGES: WINTER NEAR
THE NORTHEAST ENTRANCE

BISON

RED FOX

COW ELK

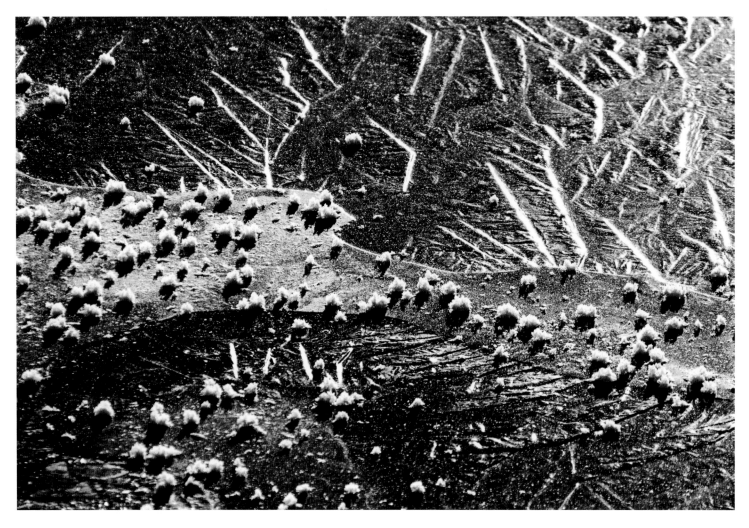

ICE PATTERN ON SODA BUTTE CREEK

WINTER IN LAMAR VALLEY

OLD FAITHFUL

ELK ON THE BLACKTAIL PLATEAU

PRONGHORN

LODGEPOLE PINES

SYLVAN LAKE

GRAY JAY

WOLF

LAMAR VALLEY

HARLEQUIN LAKE

BISON IN LAMAR VALLEY

GOLDEN EAGLE

YELLOW-BELLIED
MARMOT

MULE DEER DOE

SUMMIT OF MOUNT WASHBURN

SYLVAN LAKE

SUNRISE AT SWAN LAKE FLATS

BULL ELK ALONG THE MADISON RIVER
FOLLOWING PAGES: YELLOWSTONE LAKE

YELLOWSTONE RIVER AND CALCITE SPRINGS

BIGHORN SHEEP ABOVE THE YELLOWSTONE RIVER

MAIN TERRACE, MAMMOTH HOT SPRINGS

"BOBBY SOCKS" TREES, LOWER GEYSER BASIN

BOARDWALK, UPPER GEYSER BASIN

BISON NEAR MAMMOTH HOT SPRINGS

PORCELAIN BASIN

ORANGE SPRING MOUND,
MAMMOTH HOT SPRINGS

ELK AT SWAN LAKE FLATS

ABOUT THE PHOTOGRAPHER

Christopher Cauble grew up in Helena, Montana, where he began his passion for photography by exploring the local mountains with a 35mm film camera passed down from his parents. After graduating from the University of Montana with a bachelor's degree in geography, he became a freelance photographer working mostly in Montana and Yellowstone National Park. His work has been featured in magazines and books, including *A Montana Journal* and the popular children's book, *What I Saw In Yellowstone*. Cauble is also a dedicated nature cinematographer and his videos have been published on many national and international news sites and television programs. He lives near Yellowstone in Livingston, Montana, with his wife, Sarah. His work can be found on his website, www.caublephotography.com and on social media.

ACKNOWLEDGMENTS

I am grateful to the National Park Service and its dedicated rangers and biologists for their work and research in preserving Yellowstone National Park. Also for the books, maps, and programs of the Yellowstone Association that have been invaluable in expanding my knowledge of all aspects of Yellowstone.

I would not have such a deep, abiding love for wild places without the early influence of my parents, who took me to Yellowstone at an early age. I want to thank them for a lifetime of guidance, patience, and for always believing in me. Additionally, I'm fortunate to be surrounded by wonderful family and friends who continue to inspire me. And especially, I am forever grateful to my beautiful wife, Sarah. I want to thank her for her endless love, support, and encouragement, and whose design skills helped make this book come to life.